Come Emmanuel

Ann Lewin is one of today's most popular spiritual writers and is greatly in demand as a retreat leader. She taught English and RE in secondary schools and was later Welfare Adviser for International Students at the University of Southampton. She has also worked as a local tutor with students on the Ordination course based at Sarum College, Salisbury.

Come Emmanuel

Approaching Advent,
Living with Christmas

Ann Lewin

CANTERBURY
PRESS

Norwich

© Ann Lewin 2012

This edition published in 2012 by Canterbury Press

Editorial office
3rd floor, Invicta House
108–114 Golden Lane
London ECIY OTG

Canterbury Press is an imprint of Hymns Ancient and Modern Ltd
(a registered charity)
13a Hellesdon Park Road, Norwich, Norfolk, NR6 5DR

www.canterburypress.co.uk

British Library Cataloguing in Publication data

A catalogue record for this book is available from the British
Library

978 1 84825 207 3

Typeset by Manila Typesetting Company
Printed and bound by
CPI Group (UK) Ltd, Croydon, CRO 4YY

Contents

Introduction

Advent:
a time for discovering
treasure in darkness;
Christmas:
the dawn of light
transforming life.

Writing is often a matter of bringing out of the storehouse treasures old and new. I have drawn on material already published in *Watching for the Kingfisher* (Canterbury Press 2009), and *Seasons of Grace*, (Canterbury Press 2010). All quotations from Scripture are taken from the NRSV. Other sources are acknowledged in notes accompanying the text.

Advent and Christmas are seasons rich in symbolism, and I am grateful for this opportunity to share my exploration of them. I want to thank Christine Smith, editor at Canterbury Press, and her colleagues, for their encouragement, and Gary Philbrick who read the script in preparation and made helpful comments.

Using the material

I hope the book will provide food for thought and fresh ideas for worship for both individuals and groups. The Bible readings we hear and the hymns we sing at this time of the year can be so familiar that we sometimes miss the impact of their message. I hope that this book will be of help to all who prepare and lead services during Advent and Christmas.

Because the last ten days or so before Christmas are often busy with Carol Services and Nativity Plays, groups might find it helpful to begin meeting in November and avoid over-load in the immediate run-up to the Festival. Ideally, every member of a group should have a copy of the book, so that the relevant chapter can be read before each meeting. But in order to facilitate participation by people who have not been able to prepare in this way, it would be helpful for one per-son to spend up to fifteen minutes introducing the material for discussion. A summary could also be provided, so that members of the group have material to think about during a period of about fifteen minutes for quiet reflection. At the end of this time, to help people who are not used to group discussion to get involved, it might be helpful to suggest that each member of the group talks with another for a few min-utes, before opening discussion up to the whole group. Each chapter except the first (which for this purpose should be linked with the second chapter) ends with suggestions for pondering and prayer, and these could form the basis for some follow-up to the meeting. Each meeting should last no longer than an hour and a half including time for refresh-ments, and should finish with a short time of prayer.

The Advent chapters would provide material for 6 sessions:

Session 1, Chapters 1 and 2: Introducing Advent
Session 2, Chapter 3: The Antiphons
Session 3, Chapter 4: Wisdom
Session 4, Chapter 5: Look to your roots
Session 5, Chapter 6: Look to the future
Session 6, Chapter 7: God with us.

During the Christmas period, it is unlikely that groups would meet but, after Twelfth Night, it might be appropriate to meet again and use the remaining material in the time before Lent, to explore what difference Christmas has made to our lives, and how we can carry the Light of Christ into the rest of the year.

People who use the book individually might find it helpful to link up with another person to discuss what they have discovered.

Ann Lewin
Southampton 2012

I

Advent

The season of Advent has been observed in many different ways through the centuries. There is some evidence that in the Eastern Church, before the Nativity of Christ was observed on 25 December, the six weeks leading up to 6 January were kept as a period of preparation for Baptism, and were marked by fasting and prayer. The Eastern Orthodox Churches still observe the Nativity on 6 January. In the West, by the time of Gregory the Great, bishop in Rome in the sixth century, Advent had become a time of preparation for the celebration of the Nativity on 25 December, still marked by fasting and prayer.

The Latin word *adventus,* from which our word Advent comes, is paralleled in Greek by the word *parousia,* which has strong links, in Christian tradition, with the expectation of Christ's second coming in judgement. For several centuries, as people familiar with the Book of Common Prayer will recognize, people's thoughts were directed to contemplation of the Four Last Things: Death, Judgement, Hell and Heaven. The Book of Common Prayer collect set for use every day in Advent kept worshippers focused on the idea of judgement:

Almighty God, give us grace to cast away the works of darkness, and put upon us the armour of light, now in the time of this mortal life, in which thy Son Jesus Christ came to visit us in great humility; that in the last day, when he shall come in his glorious Majesty to judge both the quick and the dead, we may rise to the life immortal, through him who liveth and reigneth with thee and the Holy Ghost, now and ever. Amen

In recent years there has been a shift away from that focus towards joyful expectation of Christ's coming at Christmas, the embodiment of God's saving work in liberating his people from oppression. The Lectionary readings in this season remind us of the hope that God will finally vindicate his people, when the Day of the Lord comes. But that day as the prophets remind us will be a day of judgement, and God requires of us faithful obedience to his law now, demonstrated by concern and action for justice and peace. As the celebration of Christ's birth draws nearer, John the Baptist reiterates the need for a change of heart: repentance is not only a matter of confessing sin, but includes amendment of life. In the physical world darkness grows, in the Northern Hemisphere at least, but as we move towards the shortest day, in our spiritual journey the light becomes more intense, as Mary and Joseph, in obedience to God's call, enable the child who is to be the Light of the world to be born.

The weeks after Christmas, leading up to Candlemas, offer us as much food for thought as the days of preparation in Advent. Celebrating Christmas is the culmination of the preparation, but not the end of the story, for the light goes on spreading. The days after Christmas plunge us into the conflict between light and darkness that John expresses powerfully in his Gospel. The feast of the first martyr, Stephen, the Slaughter of the Innocents, the naming of Jesus, the visit of the Magi, the Baptism of Jesus, the wedding at Cana take us back and forth through Christ's growing into his ministry with scant regard for chronology, but all the strands of prophecy from the Old Testament lead into the recognition by Simeon and Anna that this child is the light for the Gentiles as well as the glory of God's people Israel.

2

Living in two worlds

Wachet auf

Advent.
Season when dual citizenship
holds us in awkward tension.

The world, intent on
spending Christmas,
eats and drinks its way to
oblivion after dinner.
The Kingdom sounds
insistent warnings:
Repent, Be ready,
Keep awake, He comes.

Like some great fugue
the themes entwine:
the Christmas carols
demanding our attention
in shops and pubs,
bore their insistent way
through noise of traffic;
underneath, almost unheard,
the steady, solemn theme of
Advent.

With growing complexity,
clashing, blending,
rivals for our attention,
themes mingle and separate,
pulling us with increasing urgency,
until in final resolution,
the end attained,
harmony rests in aweful stillness,
and the child is born.

He comes, both Child and Judge.
And will he find us watching?

(from *Watching for the Kingfisher*)

Advent is a special time in the Church's year, but it is also difficult to observe, because we are being pulled in different directions. The music that inspired that poem, Bach's Chorale Prelude *Wachet Auf*, evokes the season for us: the dancing notes above the sonorous melody represent the world around us getting caught up in the Christmas rush; underneath, the solemn tune reminds us of the Advent call to wait, prepare, get ready to greet the one who comes as Child and Judge.

The commercial world will be keen to tell us how many *shopping* days there are before the festival. The Church reminds us that the same number of *praying* days remain. How can we make good use of these praying days? There are so many demands on us as the Christmas rush gathers momentum, that suggesting that we spend more time in prayer may seem like a demand too far. But prayer is not just about the time we set aside to focus our attention on God. Prayer is the life blood of our relationship with God, a relationship that continues through all our activities and dealings with others. We miss the point if we dismiss all that is going on around us as irrelevant to the real meaning of Christmas. The real meaning of Christmas is that God came into the world and got involved in all that human life is engaged in. Advent is a time for us to embody that truth in the way that we live, so that we establish more firmly the habit of finding God in all that we do, in order to carry the practice on more consistently throughout the year.

Ponder and pray

Most of us will spend time in shops during Advent. *Shopping* may seem a rather unlikely context for prayer, but it holds great possibilities. In the supermarket, for example, there are many opportunities. As we look along the shelves, we can think about all the people who have worked to produce the goods we want to buy, and give thanks for them. We can think about those who are exploited by people with power, and ask forgiveness for our misuse of human as well as material resources. We can actively seek out goods that are fairly traded, and give thanks for all who work to challenge unfair practices. We could perhaps ask why the shops we are in don't do more to promote fairly traded goods. When we are waiting in the queue to check out, instead of being irritated by the delay, we can pray for others waiting with us, asking God's blessing on them. If we manage to spread a little calm by our demeanour, we may when we reach the till be able to say something encouraging to the person operating it – it might make all the difference to their day.

As we *read the paper* or *watch the news on television*, instead of getting depressed, sucked into the 'I don't know what the world is coming to' mind-set, we can put the situations which disturb us into God's hands with 'Lord have mercy' (remembering to pray for those who cause the trouble as well as their victims). And when there is good news, 'Thank God'.

Choosing presents and writing cards provide yet another opportunity, as we think of the recipients: our brief hope that all is well with them can be a prayer for them. We can extend our prayer to all who haven't got the resources to celebrate, and all for whom Christmas is a painful time.

Drawing up the guest list for celebrations may prompt us to think about inviting someone who would otherwise be alone; and we can give thanks for all who will provide food and shelter for the homeless. We will probably receive many requests for help from charities, and these can be a spur to thinking about how well our use of money reflects love for our neighbours.

There is nothing that we do that can't be an opportunity for *making the connection between God and the world*. (If there is anything we can identify, perhaps we shouldn't be doing it!) There is a story told about two monks who had an argument about whether you can drink coffee and pray at the same time. Since they couldn't agree, they thought they had better ask their spiritual directors for guidance. When they next met, they still couldn't agree. One monk said that his director had been very shocked at the thought – nothing should be allowed to distract from prayer. The other monk said his director had been very laid back about it, and wondered why he had asked. He asked the first monk what he had said, and he replied, 'I asked if it was all right to drink coffee while I was praying, and my director said I must never let anything take my attention away from my prayer.' 'Oh', said the other monk, laughing, 'I just asked if it was all right to pray while I was drinking my coffee.' There is wisdom there. And it will work with any kind of drink.

3

The Advent Antiphons

Advent is a godsend, encouraging us to stand back, observe, take time: time for prayer, not in the narrow sense of saying words, but in the deeper sense of spending time in God's company, watching, waiting, listening. Some of the words we are given to ponder during this season are found in the Advent Antiphons, meditations on verses of Scripture that were sung in turn from at least the fourth century, before and after the Magnificat at Vespers, the monastic equivalent of Evensong, on the seven days leading up to Christmas. By the twelfth century, five of these had been put together into a Latin hymn, translated into English in the nineteenth century by John Mason Neale. They form the basis of the hymn *O come, O come Emmanuel*. The first of the Antiphons survives by name in modern Lectionaries, where 17 December is named *O Sapientia*.

O Sapientia (O Wisdom)

O Wisdom, coming forth from the Most High, filling all creation and reigning to the ends of the earth: come and teach us the way of truth.

(Isaiah 11:2–3; Wisdom 7:24–28; Ecclesiasticus 1:1–20)

O **Adonai** (O Mighty Lord)

O Lord of Lords, and ruler of the House of Israel, you appeared to Moses in the fire of the burning bush, and gave him the Law on Sinai: come with your outstretched arm and ransom us.

(Isaiah 11:4–5; Exodus 3:1–6; 20:1–17)

O **Radix Jesse** (O Root of Jesse)

O Root of Jesse, standing as a sign among the nations; kings will keep silence before you for whom the nations long: come and save us and delay no longer.

(Isaiah 11:1–10; Jeremiah 33:14–16)

O **Clavis David** (O Key of David)

O Key of David and Sceptre of the House of Israel, you open and none can shut; you shut and none can open: come and free the captives from prison, and break down the walls of death.

(Isaiah 22:20–23; cf. Revelation 3:7)

O **Oriens** (O Morning Star)

O Morning Star, splendour of light eternal and bright sun of righteousness: come and bring light to those who dwell in darkness and walk in the shadow of death.

(Isaiah 9:2; 60:1–2; cf. Malachi 4:2; Luke 1:78)

O Rex Gentium (O King of the Nations)

O King of the Nations, you alone can fulfil their desires; cornerstone, binding all together: come and save the creature you fashioned from the dust of the earth.

(Isaiah 9:6; 2:4; Psalms 46,47; Jeremiah 30:8–11a)

O Emmanuel (O 'God with us')

O Emmanuel, our King and Lawgiver, hope of the nations and their saviour: come and save us, O Lord our God.

(Isaiah 7:14; 61:1–3; cf. Matthew 1:18–23; Luke 4:16–21)

The initial letters of the seven titles, read backwards, form a Latin acrostic, *Ero cras*, meaning 'Tomorrow I shall be there.'

The antiphons allude to the promises that will be embodied in the longed-for Messiah, promises we need to be effective in our own day. We are not Jewish people oppressed by a succession of foreign captors; many of us have never been persecuted for our faith, though we are aware that in some parts of the world that is the consequence of professing faith in Jesus Christ, just as it was when the New Testament *Revelation to John* was written. But we do need to be freed from oppressions that prevent peace and justice from being the established basic principles of our lives. We need to be set free from the fear of death and destruction that casts its gloom over much of the world. We need to be re-called to the great commandment to love the Lord our God with all our heart and mind and soul and strength.

These antiphons list great truths about God's nature: wisdom; the mighty Lord of the faithful; the God of history;

the one who unlocks meaning; the light banishing darkness; the king of the nations; the God who is with us – and pondering on all these will help us to recognize God alive and at large in our world. We need to remember that it was to the world, not just to the Church that God came and comes. And he doesn't come just at Christmas, or even at the Last Judgement, but *now*.

We don't only live in two worlds, the one that is going frantic all around us, and the one that lives by God's values. We operate in two time-scales: chronological time and beyond time. The point of intersection is *now*. *Now* is the time, as the Advent collect in the Book of Common Prayer puts it, for us to cast away the works of darkness, and put on the armour of light. *Now* is when we have to meet God, because we have no other time.

Ponder and pray

The hymn *O come, O come Emmanuel* is well known from the translation by John Mason Neale, of five of the antiphons found in many hymn books. Other people translated the remaining verses, which are included here, and starred.

O come, O come, Emmanuel
and ransom captive Israel,
that mourns in lonely exile here,
until the son of God appear:
Rejoice! Rejoice! Emmanuel
shall come to thee, O Israel.

* O come, thou Wisdom from on high
who orderest all things mightily;

to us the path of knowledge show,
and teach us in her ways to go.
Rejoice! Rejoice! . . .

O come, thou Rod of Jesse, free
thine own from Satan's tyranny;
from depths of hell thy people save,
and give them victory o'er the grave:
Rejoice! Rejoice! . . .

O come, thou Dayspring, come and cheer
our spirits by thine advent here;
disperse the gloomy clouds of night,
and death's dark shadows put to flight:
Rejoice! Rejoice! . . .

O come, thou Key of David, come,
and open wide our heavenly home;
make safe the way that leads on high,
and close the path to misery:
Rejoice! Rejoice! . . .

O come, O come thou Lord of Might,
who to thy tribes on Sinai's height,
in ancient times didst give the law
in cloud and majesty and awe:
Rejoice! Rejoice! . . .

* O come, thou Root of Jesse's tree
an ensign of thy people be;
before thee rulers silent fall;
all peoples on thy mercy call.
Rejoice! Rejoice! . . .

* O come, Desire of nations, bind
in one the hearts of all mankind;
bid thou our sad divisions cease,
and be thyself our King of Peace.
Rejoice! Rejoice! . . .

The contemporary American hymn writer and composer
Marty Haugen wrote another meditation on the Antiphons:

For You, O Lord, my soul in stillness waits truly my hope is in You

O Lord of light,
    our only hope of glory,
your radiance shines
    in all who look to you,
come, light the hearts of all
    in dark and shadow.
For You O Lord . . .

O Spring of Joy,
    rain down upon our spirits,
our thirsty hearts are yearning
    for your Word,
come, make us whole, be comfort
    to our hearts.
For You O Lord . . .

O Root of Life,
    implant your seed within us,
and in your advent draw us
    all to you

our hope reborn in dying
   and in rising.
For You O Lord . . .

O Key of Knowledge
   guide us in our pilgrimage,
we ever seek, yet
   unfulfilled remain,
open to us the pathway
   of your peace.
For You O Lord . . .

Come, let us bow
   before the God who made us,
let every heart be opened
   to the Lord,
for we are all the people
   of his hand.
For You O Lord . . .

Here we shall meet the Maker
   of the heavens,
Creator of the mountains
   and the seas
Lord of the stars, and present
   with us now.
For You O Lord . . .

(A musical setting for these words can be found in *Laudate*, Decani
Music 2000, no. 111)

4

Happy are those who find wisdom

O Wisdom, coming forth from the Most High, filling all creation and reigning to the ends of the earth: come and teach us the way of truth.

> Where shall wisdom be found?
> And where is the place of understanding?
> The fear of the Lord, that is wisdom;
> and to depart from evil is understanding.
>
> *(Job 28:12 and 28)*

There is a great deal in Scripture about wisdom, some contained in what is called the Wisdom Literature (Proverbs, Job, Ecclesiastes in the Old Testament, and Ecclesiasticus (or Sirach), and Wisdom in the Apocrypha), and much also in the Psalms.

Wisdom isn't the same as information or knowledge, though it includes both. Perhaps it is more to do with the way we use the understanding that we have. For example, a knowledgeable person will know that a tomato is a fruit; a wise person will tell you that it is not the best thing to put into a fruit salad. That is a trivial example: there are more profound examples we could provide, in the area of modern warfare, for instance, or in genetic engineering. Human beings can draw up plans to establish a new, modern Middle East: we have the skills, the people, the hardware to do that. But we could question the wisdom of trying to impose one way of life on another without taking full account of the history and traditions that have brought the people of that region to where they are now. Likewise, scientists have the knowledge to enable them to clone animals, including humans. Whether it is wise to use that knowledge is another matter. We could say that wisdom is what helps us to live well before God, alongside other people and the whole of creation.

How do we acquire wisdom? Scripture suggests that it is something that comes with maturity, the insight that develops over the years. Human beings grow into themselves physically, emotionally and spiritually. We don't come with a list of instructions like a pack of self-assembly furniture. We grow by using the role models we find around us. Christians have Jesus as their role model, and wisdom was one of the attributes he developed in his earthly life: Luke tells us (Luke 2:52) that as Jesus grew up, as well as growing physically, he increased in wisdom.

Wisdom isn't a commodity, a package we can get off the shelf. It is described as a way, a disposition. It is also personified as a companion who influences us so profoundly that we become wise in our turn.

> Wisdom is radiant and unfading
> and she is easily discerned
> by those who love her,
> and is found by those who seek her.
> She hastens to make herself known
> to those who desire her.
> One who rises early to seek her
> will have no difficulty,
> for she will be found sitting
> at the gate.
> To fix ones thought on her
> is perfect understanding,
> and one who is vigilant on her account

will soon be free from care,
because she goes about seeking
those worthy of her,

and she graciously appears to them
in their paths,
and meets them in every thought.

(*Wisdom 6:12–16*)

and

Wisdom is more mobile than any motion,
because of her pureness she pervades and
penetrates all things.
For she is the breath of the power of God,
and a pure emanation of the glory of
the Almighty;
therefore nothing defiled gains entrance
into her.
For she is the reflection of eternal light,
a spotless mirror of the working of God,
and an image of his goodness.
Although she is but one, she can do
all things,
and while remaining in herself, she renews
all things;
in every generation she passes into
holy souls
and makes them friends of God,
and prophets;
for God loves nothing so much as
the person who lives with wisdom.

(*Wisdom 7:24–28*)

Wisdom is a gift. Perhaps the best known embodiment of it is the gift given to King Solomon in answer to his prayer, and the way in which he applied it (1 Kings 3:5–28). Where shall we find it, or how shall we dispose ourselves to receive it? Job came to the conclusion that the place to start is to live in the fear of the Lord. Living in that fear is not the same as having the fear of God put into you: it is not the kind of fear that paralyses. It is perhaps better understood as living with an attitude of awe and reverence that takes God seriously (but not too solemnly).

Like many of God's gifts, we receive it in part from other human beings. Some wisdom we inherit from the past, timeless wisdom that has stood the test, always true. Many of us will have learnt proverbs as children: 'a stitch in time saves nine', 'many hands make light work', and so on. Jesus would have learnt the equivalent values from his parents – the books of wisdom would have been part of his study. Other kinds of wisdom we realize have to be challenged. We sometimes talk about 'received wisdom', and when we do, we are usually expressing some doubt about what seemed to be true at one time, but doesn't sit easily with our understanding now. For example, it used to be thought perfectly acceptable to enslave people. But then came people who challenged that concept, and established a wiser approach to treating people from other cultures and races.

We need to draw on the wisdom of previous generations, and apply it in the light of contemporary understanding of what it is to be human. That is what Jesus kept on doing. The Gospels record him telling stories that illustrated people's lives and relationships. Sometimes he said, 'Go and do the same' (Luke 10:25–37); at other times he said 'Think, see what conclusions you draw' (Matthew 6:26–34). At yet other times he said 'That old idea won't do. You have heard it said, "Love your neighbour and hate your enemy", but

I say to you "Love your enemies, and pray for those who persecute you"' (Matthew 5:17–48).

On one occasion we see him rising to the challenge himself, in his encounter with the Canaanite woman who came seeking healing for her daughter who was ill. The received wisdom of the time among the Jews was that Gentiles were not worth bothering about – they were beyond God's concern. But when Jesus saw the woman's faith, and encountered her spirited claim to be worth noticing, he responded by granting her desire, and her daughter was healed. One instance, perhaps, of Jesus increasing in wisdom (Matthew 15:21–28).

Biblical wisdom revolves around the idea that we need to live our lives in awareness of God, accountable to God, in a context of reverent worship. That comes about when we decide that our priority is to love God with all our heart, mind, soul and strength. Jesus did that, and it showed in the way he paid attention to God in prayer and public worship, in the way he treated people with profound respect, and the way he recognized God's faithful love in sustaining the whole creation. That's not a bad description of how we too can begin to live in the fear of God, and grow in wisdom, as we live in growing awareness of God, rooting that awareness in prayer, which is the heartbeat of our relationship with God.

Ponder and pray

A tried and trusted way of pondering the word of God is the practice of *Lectio Divina* (sacred reading). It is not Bible study with a commentary, but a way of letting Scripture speak to us through slow, meditative reading of a passage, letting the words sink in. We may need to read the chosen passage more than once. When a word or phrase demands our attention, we pause and stay with it as long as it feels right. We may feel moved to make some response of adoration, penitence or commitment, or simply enjoy being in God's presence.

When it feels time to move on, it is appropriate to give thanks to God for whatever we have received. We may not feel we have received anything much, but God will have been at work in the depths of our being, and we may well become aware of the blessing of his presence later.

A prayer of St Benedict

Gracious and Holy Father,
Give us wisdom to perceive you,
diligence to seek you,
patience to wait for you,
eyes to behold you,
a heart to meditate on you,
and a life to proclaim you,
through the power of the Spirit
of Jesus Christ our Lord.
Amen.

5

Look to your roots

O Adonai (O Mighty Lord)

> O Lord of Lords and ruler of the House of Israel, you appeared to Moses in the fire of the burning bush, and gave him the Law on Sinai: come with your outstretched arm and ransom us.

This antiphon reminds us of a thread that runs through the whole of Scripture: the thread of God's action in leading people from slavery to freedom, intertwined with his faithful care in good times and bad.

God's claim to be the mighty Lord, with authority over the people simply because he is as he is, finds expression in many places in Scripture. Here the antiphon takes us to God's meeting with Moses in the mysteriously burning bush (Exodus 3:1–6), when God reminds Moses that he has always been God for his people since the time of Abraham, and always works for their deliverance from oppression. God's promise to Abraham to make his descendants a great nation had been frustrated, but God had continued to work through their history whether the people deserved it or not. He used some fairly shady characters, as well as the more obviously righteous, to move his purpose forward and bring positive outcomes from some unpromising situations. Think of Jacob, a deceitful schemer if ever there was one, and his youngest son, Joseph, who was not a pleasant person in his youth. Joseph had insight into his own potential, but not much wisdom in suggesting to his brothers that they would all owe allegiance to him in the future. But in the end, he recognized that all his good fortune was to be attributed to God: the key verse in his gripping saga (Genesis 37−47) comes when he says to his brothers who have just realized with whom they are dealing, 'It was not you who brought me here but God' (Genesis 45:8). He saw God's hand in his rescue from the pit his brothers had dug for him, and his subsequent rise to importance in Egypt. When it came to Egypt's turn to be defeated, it would be the God of Abraham, Isaac and Jacob who would use Moses to bring his people out of Egypt. It was this event, the Exodus, that God gave as his reason for giving his people the laws that would guide their lives. (Exodus 20:1−17; Deuteronomy 5:1−21). God's relationship with his people was a covenanted relationship, a relationship in which both parties pledged faithfulness to each other, that made demands on the people in return for God's faithful care.

O Radix Jesse (O Root of Jesse)

O Root of Jesse, standing as a sign among the nations; kings will keep silence before you for whom the nations long: come and save us and delay no longer.

One of the high spots in the people's story was the reign of David, son of Jesse, flawed though he was: adultery and murder were hardly the best qualifications for being singled out as a great leader. The history of the people of God had its ups and downs, but, in David's reign, the people became more securely established in their land, and subsequent

generations looked back to his time as a golden age, a fore-
taste of what would happen when God came to save his
people from oppression. This hope became focused on the
Messiah, who would come from David's line, and filled
with God's Spirit would establish peace and justice on the
earth (Isaiah 11:1–3; Jeremiah 33:14–16). The prophets,
speaking often against a background of despair, spoke of
a new age, when God's covenanted relationship with his
people would be renewed (Jeremiah 31:31–34; Micah
4:1–5) but it would require a change of heart on the people's part – a renewal associated with judgement (Malachi
3:4–end).

We are reminded by this antiphon that longing for God's
kingdom to come is not a nostalgic longing for the return
of a golden age. Perhaps there never was one. It's easy to
think that things were better in years gone by, and wish
we could return to that state. Think of this description of
society:

> The world is passing through troubled times. The young
> people of today think of nothing but themselves. They
> have no reverence for parents or old age. They are im-
> patient of all restraint. They talk as if they knew every-
> thing, and what passes as wisdom with us is foolishness
> with them. As for the girls, they are foolish and immod-
> erate in speech, behaviour and dress.

If that sounds familiar, it is salutary to realize that it was
written by Peter the Monk in 1274 (Information from the
internet: http//www.edges.tv).

We can't cling on to the past, real or imagined, as though
that were the only way to stay close to God. 'As it was in the
beginning, is now and ever shall be' is part of a statement

about the appropriateness of giving glory to God, not a formula for keeping things as they have always been. Tradition is something that evolves to meet the demands of the current context. It must never be allowed to become a straitjacket that prevents us from engaging with the real world. That's true of ways of worship, as well as in other areas of life. We can commit idolatry by clinging on to old familiar ways of worship just as much as by making our own version of God. Lucy Winkett, referring to Evensong in St Paul's Cathedral, where she was Precentor for a time, commented that it is sometimes a little difficult to resist the feeling that we are in some kind of ecclesiastical version of the Sealed Knot Society, re-enacting events from the seventeenth century for our own enjoyment. (Lucy Winkett, *Our Sound is our Wound*, London: Continuum, 2010, p. 32)

Advent challenges us to look at how God has dealt faithfully with us in our personal and corporate lives, often bringing positive good out of unpromising situations, and to respond in thanksgiving, using that recognition to deepen our trust in God whose desire is always our good, to look for ways in which God is at work now, and to have the courage to change in order to co-operate with him. As God was in the beginning, God is now, and always will be, and God is worthy of our trust.

One of the great heroes of the church was Polycarp, a Bishop in Smyrna in Asia in the second century. He was martyred in AD 155, during one of the fiercest persecutions the church experienced. When it was clear that the people were after him, he wanted to stay in the city, but his friends persuaded him to leave and seek safety. He went to a farm not far from the city, and spent his time with his companions in prayer, not for himself, but as his custom was, for the people of the world, and the churches in their mission to them. His respite was short lived, and his pursuers caught up with him quite late on a Friday evening. He ordered that they should be given food and drink, and asked them to give him an hour for prayer. In fact, he prayed for two hours. And those who witnessed his prayer began to feel ashamed that they had come after so venerable an old man.

He was taken back into the city and, throughout the journey, his captors tried to persuade him to say 'Caesar is Lord', and so save himself. But he refused even to think of it. He was brought to the stadium, and asked formally to swear allegiance to Caesar and curse Christ. His response was to say, 'Eighty-six years I have served him, and he has done me no wrong. How then can I blaspheme my king who saved me?'

Ponder and pray

Whatever our age, we can all say that of God's faithfulness: in all my years, God has done me no wrong. We may not be able to thank God *for* everything that happens to us – but we can thank God for his faithful love *in* everything. He never lets us go.

*Spend some time looking back over your own experience, and the experiences of your family and community, and give thanks to God for his faithfulness.

*Write your own thanksgiving prayer.

6

Look to the future

O Clavis David (O Key of David)

O Key of David and Sceptre of the House of Israel, you open and none can shut; you shut and none can open: come and free the captives from prison, and break down the walls of death.

O Oriens (O Morning Star)

O Morning Star, splendour of light eternal and bright sun of righteousness: come and bring light to those who dwell in darkness and walk in the shadow of death.

O Rex Gentium (O King of the Nations)

O King of the Nations, you alone can fulfil their desires: cornerstone, binding all together: come and save the creature you fashioned from the dust of the earth.

Anchoring our faith in the God who has always been faithful helps us to look more confidently to the future. These antiphons remind us of God's power to deliver us from all that oppresses us, whether in physical, practical terms, or in our inner world where the darkness of ignorance and fear imprisons us.

During this season, readings from Scripture will point us to God's work through the Patriarchs and Prophets offering his people, in the course of many centuries, a living relationship with himself. But it is not a cosy relationship, for God made a Covenant with his people right at the beginning, that required obedience to his Law. Prayer that God will deliver us from all that mars our relationship with him will recall us to the need for a change of heart on our part.

Our contemporary observance of Advent has moved away from the Book of Common Prayer's attention to the Four Last Things: Death, Judgement, Heaven and Hell. But the antiphons remind us that Judgement plays a real part in calling us back to the need for repentance. And the time for that is *now*, we do not have to let things ride until the Last Day. The Prophets made it very clear that the Day of the Lord that people longed for was not going to be a day when God's people would be able to gloat over their enemies because God had at last shown how special his people were to him. The Day of the Lord would be a day of judgement for all people, and each person would be held accountable for their actions. The teaching of Amos exemplifies this well: after running through all that the neighbouring nations had done wrong, Amos turned to the people of Judah and Israel and spelled out their destiny (Amos 1:2–3, 2; 7:7–9). His description of the Day of the Lord makes it quite clear that it will not be a day of delight:

Alas for you who desire the day of the Lord!
Why do you want the day of the Lord?
It is darkness, not light;
as if someone fled from a lion,
and was met by a bear;

or went into a house
and rested a hand against a wall,
and was bitten by a snake.
Is not the day of the Lord darkness, not light,
and gloom with no brightness in it?

(Amos 5:8–20)

The worship the people offer is a travesty of worship because it does not reflect the standards God had set, standards of justice and mercy. God is not impressed with lavish
religious ceremonies offered by people whose lives do not
reflect the worship they offer:

I hate, I despise your festivals,
and I take no delight in your
solemn assemblies.
Even though you offer me your
burnt offerings and your grain offerings
I will not accept them,
and the offerings of well-being of
your fatted animals
I will not look upon.
Take away from me the noise of your songs;
I will not listen to the melody of your harps.
But let justice roll down like the waters,
and righteousness like an
ever-flowing stream.

(Amos 5:21–24)

In medieval times people were reminded of the judgement
that awaited them by the Doom paintings set above the
chancel arch in their churches. One of the best preserved
of these is in The Church of St Thomas and St Edmund in

Salisbury (for an illustration, visit www.Stthomassalisbury.
co.uk). Above the centre of the arch sits Christ in majesty,
with the apostles and other blessed ones surrounding him.
On the left the dead are emerging from their tombs, on the
right those destined for Hell are being pitchforked into the
flames by a gleeful demon. All are brought before the judgement seat naked as they were born, except for a bishop who
is wearing his mitre. He may have been given that to save his
dignity, but it reminds us that we are all responsible for our
own actions, and some of us, all of us to some degree, are
responsible for the way other people are enabled to respond
to God in their daily circumstances, and will be judged for
the way we have used that responsibility. The prophets had
made that point: Amos had spoken about lifestyles that con-
demned others to poverty of different kinds (Amos 2:6–8);
Jeremiah and Ezekiel spoke out about the way the leaders
of the people had abused their position (Jeremiah 23:1–6;
Ezekiel 18 and 34:1–16). Those who were being sent to Hell
in the Salisbury Doom painting carried with them symbolic
evidence of the reason for their destiny: for example, an ale-
wife brandishes the jug from which she had presumably dis-
pensed short measure.

John the Baptist, the last in the line of those whose work
it was to prepare people for the coming of the Messiah,
also gave an uncompromising message about the need for
repentance, a change of heart. When particular groups of
people asked him for guidance about the form that repentance should take, he gave it in the same terms as the Old
Testament prophets had done – justice and mercy are the
keynotes of the Kingdom, the very stuff of the wisdom that
enables us to live in the right relationship with God and
each other (Luke 3:2–14).

As in our Northern hemisphere the days grow darker,
moving to the shortest day on 21 December, in Advent

the promise of light grows stronger. The coming of God in judgement, and the need for repentance that will set us free through God's forgiveness, is set alongside the coming of God to enlighten us with his life-giving Word, Jesus the Light of the World. It was Mary who, with Joseph, co-operated with God to enable the light to be brought to birth. It has not always been easy to disentangle Mary from doctrinal statements and devotional adulation often fuelled by artists' portrayals of her, so that we can see her as a helpful role model for ordinary Christians.

You always appear
Too good to be true, Mary.
We've pictured you always serene,
Never exasperated by a fractious child,
Apparently having no feelings.

But surely that initial Yes came
From a moment of overwhelming terror?
And the birth tore you to the core?
Did he never cry, that baby,
Give you sleepless nights?
Didn't he irritate you,
That precocious son
Dismissing your anxiety with
Didn't you know? And later
That wounding question,
Who is my mother?
My mother would have told him . . .
Perhaps you did too,
But it wasn't recorded.

Even at the end, you're pictured
Beautiful in your sorrow,

Holding your dead child.
Not like those ravaged faces
We see on our screens
Raging at the senseless
Killing of the innocent.

(*Get Real*, from *Watching for the Kingfisher*)

Mary was the agent of the 'New thing' that God was doing, promised in the words of Isaiah (Isaiah 43:19). The fulfilment of the promise had been delayed through people's unwillingness to co-operate with God and live by his laws. But now, the time is right (as New Testament writers later understood: Galatians 4:4–5; Hebrews 1:1–2a), and Mary's 'Yes' is the signal for the beginning of the establishment of the Kingdom. Portraying Mary as a meek virgin doesn't help those who are neither, nor does it do her justice: her Magnificat (Luke 1:46–55) indicates that she was a feisty woman with a real concern for justice. It was her attentiveness to God that led to her becoming the one through whom God's purpose could be brought to birth. Among all the artistic portrayals of Mary, perhaps the most helpful to ponder on is *The Annunciation* by Michelangelo, where Mary is shown at prayer.

It was not the first time
You had been there waiting, wondering.
This time there was quickening of senses,
Certainty that you would give birth.
A flash of insight, filling you with terror,
How could this be?

The disconcerting messenger insisted
What you would bear was gift of God.

No need to wonder how,
The gift you needed was already in you,
Slowly maturing to the point of birth.

No one told you then how birth is painful
Creation tearing you to the core.
That would come later. For the present
All that's needed is your 'Yes'.

(*Annunciation*, from *Watching for the Kingfisher*)

All that's needed is our 'Yes', too, so that we become agents, perhaps midwives, for the Kingdom of God that we pray for. The prayer of intercession is our chance to say yes to God in our turn. When we pray for God's Kingdom to come, we are not so much praying for God's intervention to solve all the problems we see around us, as offering ourselves in his service, saying that we want to put our energy alongside his energy in bringing about the change of heart that will be needed in human beings if the Kingdom is to come. We are not always keen on change: the Advent challenge is to see change as an opportunity to say 'Yes', to manage change rather than be overwhelmed by it. It will involve us in the life of our communities in political action with or without a capital letter. And it will begin with each one of us, as we respond to God's call to join in the proclamation of the Kingdom.

Ponder and pray

Spend some time with a map of the world, thinking about the situations that cause concern. Are there any actions we could take, by writing letters to politicians, by joining in campaigns for justice, by challenging misuse of power, by providing local help to people in need?

A litany for the world

In the places of decision making
And the places of powerlessness,
Come Lord let your love be known . . .

In the places of wealth
And the places of poverty,
Come Lord . . .

Where we are healthy
And where we are sick,
Come, Lord . . .

In the streets of plenty
And in the dark corners and alleys,
Come, Lord . . .

Where people are oppressed
and in the hearts of the oppressors,
Come, Lord . . .

In our places of worship
And where there is no faith,
Come, Lord . . .

In our places of learning,
And in the depths of our ignorance,
Come, Lord . . .

In our homes and our welcomes,
And where people couldn't care less,
Come, Lord . . .

We pray that in all that we are and do and say and think, we may be agents of God's Kingdom, as we say, **Our Father . . .**

(from *Seasons of Grace*, p. 33)

7

God with us

O Emmanuel, our King and Lawgiver, hope of the nations and their saviour: come and save us, O Lord our God.

> Christians awake! Salute the happy morn,
> whereon the Saviour of the world was born;
> rise to adore the mystery of love,
> which hosts of angels chanted from above;
> with them the joyful tidings first begun
> of God incarnate and the Virgin's Son.

(*J. Byrom 1692–1763*)

People sometimes say, 'Christmas is for the children.' And in one sense they are right – children are certainly centre stage. But Christmas is certainly not for the children if what we mean is that it's something we grow out of as we grow older. On the contrary, it's something we are called to grow into. We might have ended up just with a children's festival at Christmas if we had only got the Gospels of Matthew and Luke to rely on – they are the Gospels that tell us all the birth stories which we enjoy hearing each year. But a lot more was going on than what we sing about in the carols centring on the stable.

Perhaps it's significant that it's *on the third day* of Christmas that we are given the opportunity to celebrate the work of St John the Evangelist. It is on another third day that we begin to understand what God has been doing in Jesus. We don't fully understand Christmas until we have experienced Easter. John doesn't say anything in his Gospel about Bethlehem, angels, shepherds or wise men. He says, 'In the beginning was the Word, and the Word was with God, and the Word became flesh.' Jesus was the light that came into the world – he is the one who enlightens us about God – and the good news is that the world's darkness, although it can be very dark, has never extinguished that light. John's Gospel, like all the others, tells us that the child grew up, and stretched people into new maturity by what he said and did, and the person he was. We know that the only reason we keep Christmas is that it is about far more than the story of the birth of a child. And we know that we are caught up into the story when we follow Christ, because we are called out of darkness to live in the light (1 Peter 2:9).

The church gives us three days to observe straight after Christmas: St Stephen, St John and the Holy Innocents. They often get rather overlooked as we recover from the celebrations of Christmas Day. But they all illustrate the same truth about God coming into God's world. John said in his first letter 'God is light, and in him is no darkness' (1 John 1:5). But light is not always an easy thing to cope with. In his Gospel, at the end of the conversation between Jesus and Nicodemus, the man who came out of the darkness to try to find out more about Jesus, John talks about the coming of light being the point of judgement, 'Light has come into the world, and people loved darkness rather than light, because their deeds were evil' (John 3:1–21). That's what Christmas is all about – much stronger stuff than the little Lord Jesus safely asleep in the hay.

John's day is flanked by two days of harsh reality. St Stephen, the first Christian martyr, was stoned to death because he challenged the religious people of his day to let the light of Christ transform their lives. Their response was to do their best to extinguish the light by killing Stephen.

On Holy Innocents' Day we remember the babies slaughtered by Herod who couldn't bear to think of a rival usurping his position when he heard the Wise Men ask where the one born to be King of the Jews was to be found.

We may not observe either of these days with much enthusiasm, but they are there, and they nudge us into thinking about our response. It was the religious people of his day who refused the enlightenment that Jesus came to bring. Are we always keen to welcome Christ's challenge? We're not going to order the death of a lot of babies like Herod did. But what about the slaughter of present-day innocents – those children with swollen bellies, skin stretched over grinning skulls, who look at us hopelessly from our TV screens. Are we not in some way responsible for them? John says that if, right in the middle of the nastiness that human beings are capable of, if we say that we are God's people but go on walking in darkness, then we are not speaking the truth about our allegiance. Our fellowship with God, our friendship Jesus called it, has to make a difference. And God will make a difference in our lives if we admit to our darkness. The only people God can't do anything with are those who say they don't need him. 'If we say that we have no sin, we deceive ourselves, and the truth is not in us. If we confess our sin, he is faithful and just, and will forgive our sins and cleanse us from all unrighteousness' (1 John 1:6–7). It's a very business-like statement. John doesn't say we have to wallow in guilt, he says confess, and be forgiven. And then we have to learn to live as forgiven people. Recognizing who we are, and our need for God, is the challenge we all have to face. It's the challenge the Word made flesh gives to us all, and the challenge becomes sharper as the Word grows up into adulthood.

The birth of Jesus was not the happy ending to the longing that God's people had for God to come and save them. It was the focusing of the struggle between light and darkness that would reach its decisive battle at the Cross, and its resolution with the Resurrection. We sometimes hear people say, when the preparations for Christmas get too demanding, that they will be glad when it's all over. But it is never over. Christmas can't be put away with the decorations until next year. Christmas stays with us, and sets the agenda for our Christian living.

Incarnation

He's grown, that Baby.
Not that most people have noticed,
He still looks the same,
Lying there in the straw, with
Animals and shepherds looking on.
He's safe there, locked in that moment
Where time met Eternity.

Reality of course is different,
He grew up. Astonished people with his
Insight, disturbed them with
Ideas that stretched them into
New maturity.

Some found him
Much too difficult to cope with,
Nailed him down to fit their
Narrow minds.

We are more subtle,
Keep him helpless,
Refuse to let him be the Man he is,
Adore him as the Christmas Baby

Eternally unable to grow up
Until we set him free.

By all means let us pause there
At the stable, and
Marvel at the miracle of birth.
But we'll never get to know
God with us, until we learn
To find him at the Inn,
A fellow guest who shares the joy and sorrow,
The Host who is the life we celebrate.

He's grown, that Baby.

(from *Watching for the Kingfisher*)

Ponder and pray

Christmas is the season to pause at the stable, and marvel at God's love. The kind of prayer that we call Contemplation is a very simple form of prayer. It may have a rather grand name, but it is not a specialist activity undertaken by people who are specially holy. It corresponds to the stage in a relationship when we don't need to talk, but can simply be with another person enjoying their company, and letting them enjoy being with us. Reaching this stage in our relationship with God may take years, because we find it hard to believe that 'God loves us and delights in us, and wants us to love him and delight in him', as Julian of Norwich said (*Revelation of Divine Love*, Short Text, Chapter 22). But Christmas is all about God loving us, and wanting to be with us. That's the truth to take into our post-Christmas break, and the rest of our lives. We might try to be still for a time each day, and let God love us.

We have to learn to be still: one way to do it is to replace all the other things we have on our minds with a rhythm prayer (sometimes called a mantra) that we can use to focus ourselves, or to bring ourselves back to God when our thoughts wander off, as they often do. We might use a short text from Scripture, 'my heart longs for you' (Psalm 42) or, 'My Lord and my God' (John 20:28). We might listen to some music to help us quieten our minds. Some more words from Julian of Norwich could be our prayer:

God of your goodness give us yourself, for you are enough for us, and if we ask for anything less we shall always be in want. Only in you we have all.

(Paraphrased from *Revelation of Divine Love*, Long Text, Chapter 5, in Julian of Norwich, *Showings*, New York: Paulist Press, 1978.)

8

On the Feast of Stephen

Good King Wenceslas looked out
on the feast of Stephen;
when the snow lay round about,
deep and crisp and even.
Brightly shone the moon that night,
though the frost was cruel;
when a poor man came in sight
gathering winter fuel.

'Hither, page, and stand by me,
if thou knowest it telling,
yonder peasant, who is he,
where and what his dwelling?'
'Sire, he lives a good league hence,
underneath the mountain,
right against the forest fence,
by St Agnes' fountain.'

'Bring me flesh, and bring me wine,
bring me pine logs hither,
thou and I will see him dine
when we bear them thither.'
Page and monarch forth they went,
forth they went together;

Through the rude wind's wild lament,
And the bitter weather.

'Sire, the night is darker now,
and the wind blows stronger.
Fails my heart, I know not how,
I can go no longer.'
'Mark my footsteps, good my page,
tread thou in them boldly;
thou shalt find the winter's rage
freeze thy blood less coldly.'

In his master's steps he trod,
Where the snow lay dinted,
Heat was in the very sod
Which the saint had printed.
Therefore, Christian men, be sure
Wealth or rank possessing
Ye who now will bless the poor,
Shall yourselves find blessing.

(J. M. Neale)

The spirit of goodwill lingers on for a while after Christmas Day, even though the commercial world is concentrating on the January sales, and Hot Cross buns have replaced Christmas cakes on the supermarket shelves.

Boxing Day, the Feast of Stephen, is a strange mixture. In part its name takes us back to the days when a Christmas Box, today we would probably call it a bonus, was given to servants and manual workers. It is a day for continuing the Christmas celebrations, with sport, family parties, eating left-overs, perhaps even getting down to writing some thank-you letters. But it is also the Feast of Stephen when, as the carol we don't sing very often now tells us, Good

King Wenceslas looked out, and encouraged his page to join him in supplying the needs of a poor man.

Stephen was chosen in the early days of the Church's history, to help look after widows, poor people who had no one to support them. He was one of the seven men 'of good standing, full of the Spirit and of wisdom', who were appointed to look after this important section of the Christian community, while the Apostles concentrated on preaching the Word (Acts 6:1–8). Stephen went further than that, though, 'he did great wonders and signs among the people'. This provoked a strong reaction among some of his fellow countrymen, who, when they challenged him, found his arguments too strong to resist. They decided to silence him, arrested him and hauled him before the Jewish Council, accusing him of blasphemy. When he was asked to give an account of himself, Stephen made a long speech giving the history of God's dealings with his people, and pointing out that throughout their history, the people had failed to listen to God. The final challenge came when God sent his Son to be his living Word, and they, his listeners, had betrayed and murdered him. That was the final straw for the Council, and they set upon Stephen, dragged him out of the city, and stoned him to death (Acts 7). One of the witnesses to this event was a young man called Saul, who would play a major role in the life of the Church later on.

There are parallels between Stephen's story and that of the jovial King of the carol. Wenceslas was a real person, son of a tenth-century Duke of Bohemia, a Christian with a pagan wife. When Wenceslas was ten, his father was killed in battle, and the young lad was given into the care of his paternal grandmother, Ludmilla, who was also a Christian. She and her daughter-in-law, Drahomira, didn't get on, and before long the grandmother was killed and Drahomira assumed the regency herself. As far as the Czech people were concerned, she was an able ruler, and secured the borders of her territory against enemies. But she didn't approve of Christianity, and tried very hard, but unsuccessfully, to convert Wenceslas back to the old religion.

When he was eighteen, Wenceslas took over the government himself, exiled his mother, and promoted the spread of Christianity throughout Bohemia. He built a cathedral, dedicated to St Vitus, in Prague. He also arranged to have his grandmother, Ludmilla, canonized as the first Czech martyr. But early in 929, Wenceslas became a vassal of a German king, and the pagan nobles, already worried by growing German influence, plotted with his younger brother Boleslav, to have Wenceslas killed. He was invited to a celebration in the cathedral, and hacked to death at the door. He was later canonized and became the patron saint of the Czech people. There is a statue of him on horseback and in armour in Wenceslas Square in Prague, though there is little historical basis for that portrayal, for he never had a military career. Outside his home country, he is best known for being the subject of our carol, written by John Mason Neale in 1875. His Feast Day is actually on 28 December, but we usually only think of him on the Feast of Stephen.

So, immediately after Christmas Day, we are faced with the harsh reality of what it can be like to take Christ seriously. The Church doesn't let us stay under the blanket of vague goodwill that permeates most of society at this time of year: as if one martyrdom isn't enough, in two days time we shall be faced with the Massacre of the Innocents. The Church reminds us that the birth of the Saviour involved pain – not just the pain of childbirth, but the pain brought about by conflict of interests, by desire for power, by selfishness. And as we trace Christ's life from the manger to the cross, we shall be reminded again and again that the baby grew up, challenged people with his insights, opened up fresh understanding, and provoked strong reactions.

Ponder and pray

Suffering presents us with perhaps the biggest challenge we ever encounter in our journey of faith. We fear it, resent it, can't make sense of it, and wonder where God is in it. We want to know why there is suffering, and why God doesn't step in to stop it. Perhaps the clues to some kind of answer lie in what we believe about God, rather than in the nature of suffering. God has given the universe laws which it has to follow, and humans freewill so that they can make their own decisions about how they live. So, in one sense suffering exists because that is the way the world is. God can't intervene without taking away those freedoms.

People sometimes wonder what they have done to deserve the suffering they experience, and the answer to that is usually, nothing. It is true that some suffering is the consequence of choices we make, and some is caused by sin: but it is not the sin of those who suffer, but of those who hold life cheap. It is quite clear from the Gospels that the God Jesus revealed does not want suffering. Jesus healed the sick, and challenged people who oppress others: 'I came that [people] may have life', he said (John 10:10).

Part of our problem lies in the language we have been accustomed to use to describe God: almighty, powerful, omnipotent. We have to enlarge our vocabulary to encompass the vulnerability of a God who has given us free will, and who knows, through the pain of the Cross, what suffering is like from the inside.

So when we come to pray, perhaps all we can do is ask God to heal the wounds of the world – recognizing that healing is not necessarily the same as cure. Healing may re-sult in the disappearance of what is troubling us, or it may mean finding fresh courage to cope with an old situation; it may be a new appreciation of our own and other people's worth; it may be a new determination to work for social justice so that the evils of oppression of various kinds may be challenged and resolved. It may seem that nothing hap-pens as a result of our prayer, but God will respond with his healing gifts at whatever level we can receive them. Then we can share them with those around.

Lord God, in your great love for your creation, fill us and all for whom we pray with your Holy Spirit. Take from us all that harms us, and make us whole in body, mind and spirit, in Jesus' name. Amen.

9

The Epiphany

On the twelfth day of Christmas the Magi arrived with their gifts, on the occasion we call The Epiphany, the revelation of the true nature of the child, the recognition of his glory. There are other epiphanies for us to observe too: there was one on 1 January, when we noted the Naming and Circumcision of Jesus. Before he was born, the special nature of this child was foretold: he is to be Emmanuel, God with us (Isaiah 7:14; Matthew 1:23). Now he has his future mapped out for him as he is called Jesus, the one who will save his people (Matthew 1:21; Luke 1:31, 2:21). Being given a name puts him on the same footing as everyone else, and places him firmly in the human race. His circumcision locates him in a particular group – and perhaps that tiny cut foreshadows the much greater shedding of blood that is to come. Later on there will be his Baptism, when the Father acknowledges his Son as he begins his ministry; and then there will be all the 'signs' that John records in his Gospel, as the true nature of Jesus' glory is revealed.

But on the twelfth day of Christmas, the Magi came with their gifts. It is a multi-layered story, as many of these birth narratives are, and three layers in particular draw our attention. First there is the nature of the visitors: Magi, astronomers from further East, led by a star to find a newly born king. They are often called Wise Men, but if we think about the nature of wisdom as the Bible describes it, that may not be the most suitable adjective to use to describe them. They were certainly clever, there is no doubt that they were well versed in the study of the stars. But perhaps if they had been wiser they would have done a little research into the nature of the King this new-born child would replace. Herod was not a popular man: he had been put in charge of the Jewish province by the Romans, and had been out of his depth from the start. He knew how fragile his hold over the people was, and it was small wonder that he was disturbed at the suggestion that someone might be in the running to succeed him. His was not a rational response – by the time a new-born baby was old enough to succeed him, Herod himself would probably be dead anyway. Perhaps the Magi picked up his agitation, and saw through his eagerness to go and pay homage to the child. At any rate, they were wise enough to listen to their dream, and go back to their own country by another route. But that did not stop Herod from doing his worst.

Another layer to ponder concerns the nature of the gifts. Gold, frankincense and myrrh were extraordinary gifts to give a child. They are of course symbolic: gold in recognition of kingship; frankincense to symbolize the priestly work Jesus would do; and myrrh foreshadowing his suffering. Gold and frankincense had been identified in prophecy (Isaiah 60:6) as gifts that would be signs of God's saving work in restoring his people. Matthew introduced myrrh as a third gift, that would be offered again when Jesus was crucified (Matthew 27:32), when a soldier offered him wine mixed with myrrh as a mild painkiller, which Jesus refused to drink; and then when Nicodemus brought a large amount of myrrh mixed with aloes as he helped Joseph of Arimathea bury Jesus' body (John 19:38-42).

Then we can think about our response, for these are gifts which we have to offer, too. Each of us is pure gold in

God's sight, 'precious, honoured and loved,' as Isaiah said (Isaiah 43:4). 'God's works of art', is the description Paul gave us (in Ephesians 2:1–10 in the Jerusalem Bible translation). What God wants is ourselves, unfinished works of art as we are, so that he can love us into wholeness. We are called to be prayerful people, deepening our relationship with God, and letting our prayerful concern for others warm the lives of people around us. Myrrh represents our willingness to enter into the suffering of humanity – sharing in Christ's suffering – bringing healing and reconciliation to the brokenness of our world.

There is nothing sentimental about our journey to make our offering. T. S. Eliot wrote memorably about the journey the Magi had. 'A cold coming we had of it', he began. He borrowed the words from a sermon preached by Lancelot Andrewes, one-time Dean of Westminster and Bishop of Chichester and Winchester, on Christmas Day 1622, in the presence of King James I. Andrewes said of the wise men:

A cold coming they had of it at this time of the year, just the worst time of the year to take a journey, and especially a long journey. The ways deep, the weather sharp, the days short, the sun farthest off, the very dead of winter. *Venimus . . .* 'we are come' . . .

And these difficulties they overcame, of a wearisome, irksome, troublesome, dangerous, unseasonable journey, and all for this they came. And came it cheerfully, and quickly, as appeareth by the speed they made. It was but *vidimus venimus*, with them 'they saw' and 'they came' no sooner saw but they set out presently . . . they took all those pains, made all this haste, that they might be here to worship Him with all the possible speed they could. Sorry for nothing so much as that they could not be there soon enough, with the very first, to do it even this day, the day of His birth. . . .

And we, what should we have done? Sure these men of the East will rise in judgement against the men of the West, that is with us, and their faith against ours in this point. With them it was but '*vidimus venimus*', with us it would have been but *veniemus* (we will come) at most. Our fashion is to see and see again before we stir a foot, specially if it be to the worship of Christ. Come such a journey at such a time? No, but fairly have put it off to the spring of the year, till the days longer, and the ways fairer, and the weather warmer, till better travelling to Christ. Our Epiphany would sure have fallen in Easter week at the soonest.

(from http//anglicanhistory.org/lact/andrewes/v1/sermon15.html)

Ponder and pray

We are challenged by the Epiphany story to think about how willing we are to set out on the journey of offering ourselves to God.

What are the gifts of Gold, Frankincense and Myrrh that we have as individuals or groups/churches to offer to God in loving our neighbours?

What obstacles do we have to overcome in order to make our offering?

Come freshly to us now, Lord God,
and as we offer you our lives,
renew in us your gifts;
the gold of our potential,
the incense of our prayers and aspirations,

the myrrh of healing for our pain;
feed us and nourish us
that we may grow in the life of Christ;
fill us with your Spirit
that we may overflow with your love,
and transform the world with your glory.

(from *A Eucharistic Prayer for The Epiphany*,
in *Seasons of Grace*, p. 47)

Endings and beginnings

When the song of the angels is stilled
When the star in the sky is gone,
When the kings and princes are home,
When the shepherds are back with their flock,
The work of Christmas begins:
To find the lost,
To heal the broken,
To feed the hungry,
To release the prisoner,
To rebuild the nations,
To make peace among the people,
To make music in the heart.

(*Howard Thurman*)

The celebration of Epiphany brings the Christmas season to an end. The cards come down, the decorations are packed away until next year, and we have to start dusting the horizontal surfaces again. But just as Christmas was not the end of the story, but the beginning of the new thing God was doing by coming to live among us in the world, the celebration of the Epiphany is the beginning of *our* continuation of the story of God's dealings with humanity. Some people keep their cribs in place for another few weeks. Whether we do so or not, we move on as more epiphanies are noted and explored. Again, there is little regard for chronology in the events to which our Bible readings for the Sundays following the Epiphany will draw our attention. (What we are given to consider depends on the date of Easter which determines how many Sundays there are between the Epiphany and the beginning of Lent.)

Mention has already been made of the Naming and Circumcision of Jesus when he was eight days old, events that rooted him in his Jewishness, and also mapped out his destiny as the Saviour Messiah. The outworking of that calling will be the subject of our exploration throughout the year.

In these weeks we are given the opportunity to consider two events at the beginning of Jesus' public life: his Baptism and the Wedding at Cana.

The Baptism of Jesus, recorded in all four Gospels (Matthew 3:13–17; Mark 1:9–11; Luke 3:1–22; John 1:19–34), introduces us to the adult Jesus beginning his ministry among people who had been drawn to want to change their lives by the preaching of his cousin John the Baptist. They had flocked out to John at the river Jordan, and made public their commitment and desire to change by being baptized. From now on, their lives would be governed by God's Law.

John made it quite clear that being baptized with water was not the full story. There was one coming who would baptize them with the Holy Spirit: their desire to change would be met by God's gift, the gift that would enable them to sustain their new commitment. It wouldn't give them the automatic right to be a part of God's Kingdom: receiving the gift carries with it the responsibility of co-operating with the Spirit in the business of change. There would still be the fact of God's judgement: the new people of God mustn't fall into the trap his ancient people had fallen into, that of thinking that they were chosen and special, and so could behave like spoilt children who could do no wrong.

Jesus came as his fellow humans had, with a desire to show his commitment to God's way. His offering of himself was accepted and honoured as he prayed after his baptism. The Spirit descended on him in visible form, and a voice from heaven said 'You are my Son, the beloved, with you I am well pleased.'

This affirmation wouldn't have come as a bolt out of the blue for Jesus. He hadn't come out to John as others had with questions about how he should change his life. He had known for some time that he must be about his Father's business – he had told his parents so when he got left behind in the Temple at twelve years old (Luke 2:41–52) This affirmation from God came as part of his prayer, his reflection on his growing sense that his mission was to meet the world's need for God's love by interpreting the people's scriptures and traditions in a way that would set them free to live as God's people, 'precious, honoured and loved' as Isaiah had said all God's people were (Isaiah 43:4). In response, God says, in effect, 'You are right, this is what it means to be my beloved.' And Jesus, filled with a fresh sense of God's Spirit, moved on to begin to work out just how he was to set about his father's business.

Most of us don't remember our baptism – we may well have been too young to be aware of what was going on. But there will have been other occasions when we have had the opportunity to make a commitment to live in God's way: at Confirmation, or at Easter ceremonies, or at particular moments very personal to ourselves when we have known deep down that what we really want is to give ourselves more completely to God. At every Communion service we offer ourselves to God afresh. And whenever we commit ourselves to God, God meets us with the gift of his life, to sustain us as we learn for ourselves what it means to be loved. That relationship with God has to be lived out in our relationships with other people, and with the whole of creation. What we have celebrated at Christmas and Epiphany is not over and done with, it is only just beginning. We are called to work with the adult Jesus in the power of God's Spirit, and to continue to grow.

What happens as we grow is the transformation of 'the poverty of our natures by the riches of God's grace', as one prayer puts it (*Collect for Epiphany 4* in the *Alternative Services Book*). That is at the heart of what happened at the Wedding in Cana, when Jesus turned what could have been a catastrophe in social terms into a life-giving experience. His presence, and the obedience of those around him, saved the day. Think of the shame and embarrassment for the host when the wine threatened to run out. Think of the amazement when the six jars, holding 20 or 30 gallons apiece, proved to contain not water but wine, and wine of such quality that all the wine people had tasted before might just as well have been water. Such is the extraordinary generosity of God's provision for his people.

It happened because the servants obeyed an instruction to do something very simple. We often want a grand gesture to effect transformation. Like Naaman the Syrian, we want an Elisha to wave his hand over us like a magic wand, rather than to be told to do something very ordinary (2 Kings 5:8–14). The servants who were told to fill the water jars may very well have thought privately that it was a fool's errand, and grumbled among themselves at the heavy work – they were big jars. But they did what they were told, and the result was beyond anyone's expectations. Ordinary water was transformed by Jesus into the source of joy and life.

This event tells us what a difference Jesus can make to our ordinary everyday experience if we let him work in us, not just in personal terms but in social terms as well. God's grace is an incredibly generous gift, but we have to be open enough to receive it. We have to be willing to share it too, because like all God's gifts it only reaches its full potential when everyone has their share. God offers us the riches of the wine of new life. We turn it back to water again when we refuse to believe that things can be different: when we let injustice continue, or are careless of human life.

Cana revisited

Can you make wine of this?
Routine of work, or lack of it;
Relationships or brokenheartedness;
Struggle to tease out meaning in the dark;
Can these be changed?
If ordinary existence
Is poured out to be used,
Could you perform
Another miracle?

Perhaps the wonder is, being faithless,
We turn the wine of our potential to
Plain water.

(from *Watching for the Kingfisher*)

Faith that God can and will make a difference is the hall-mark of the last 'epiphany' that we celebrate before we turn away from Christmas and begin to look towards the Cross and Easter, when we shall see more deeply what Christmas was all about.

For this event we have to make another illogical leap, backwards this time to the occasion, called in our church calendar The Presentation, when his parents took the six-week-old Jesus to the Temple to present him to the Lord. This was another event, like the Naming and Circumcision, that rooted Jesus firmly in the culture of his day. It was the custom according to Jewish Law to give thanks for the birth of a child, and to offer a sacrifice to mark the occasion. It was laid down (in Leviticus 12) how this should be done. But this time there was another element to what would have been a commonplace ritual, for Mary and Joseph were greeted by two people who had been longing for many years to see the fulfilment of God's promise to send a Saviour to his people. Simeon had been assured in a vision that he would not die until he had seen the Lord's Christ. Anna had devoted much of her long life since she had been made a widow, to praying in the Temple. Both of them recognized the importance of this child, and Simeon spoke, or sang, his satisfaction in words that have become a much-loved part of evening worship, the Nunc Dimittis:

Lord, now lettest thou thy servant depart in peace,
according to your word;
for mine eyes have seen thy salvation,
which thou hast prepared in the
face of all peoples,
to be a light to lighten the Gentiles
and to be the glory of thy people Israel.

(from *Evening* Prayer in the Book of Common Prayer, based on Luke 2:29–32)

Simeon can die a happy man now, for all the strands of expectation and prophecy have been drawn together in this moment. As John said in his Gospel, here was the Light of the World. For Simeon and Anna it was a senior moment to die for.

There was another aspect to the recognition Simeon expressed, for he went on to say that the child who was the light would provoke opposition from those who preferred darkness, and that Mary herself would suffer because of it. Mary had many things to keep in her heart and ponder on after the events of Jesus' birth. This was one that she would remember with pain as her child grew up.

Because Jesus was described as the Light of the World, candles have always been associated with worship, and are used as a symbol for Christ's presence. This festival is often called Candlemas, and it used to be the time when all the candles that were provided for use during the year in church would be blessed. Candles remind us that we have been called out of darkness to live in light, and it is customary now to give people who have just been baptized a candle to remind them to shine as lights in the world, to the glory of God.

Ponder and pray

This is the time when we move into preparation for Lent. Our crib figures will disappear, but Jesus the light of the world will remain with us, and will go on calling us to live with him in light. That doesn't mean that we shall be untouched by the darkness of the world, immune from sickness and suffering. But our faith is that Christ our Light is right in the middle of the darkness of the world and our lives, driving the powers of darkness back and inviting us to join our little lights to his great Light, and draw strength from him and each other.

Lord Christ, set us on fire,
Burn from us all that dims your light;

ENDINGS AND BEGINNINGS

Kindle an answering flame
In lives around,
That darkness may be driven back
And glory stream into this world,
Transforming it with light.

(from *Candlemas Prayer*, in *Watching for the Kingfisher*)

I I

Afterword

As the crib figures were being put away for another year, I found myself wondering what they had made of it all, and I thought about the conversations they might have with each other as they were packed away.

First **the Magi.** Last to arrive, and first to go into the box: perhaps they have been saddened over the years by the way they have been represented as clever people who brought exotic but apparently rather unsuitable gifts for a baby. I wonder if their conversation might be about how important it is to recognize that the gold, frankincense and myrrh are not gifts beyond the means of most of us, but the material of our attempts to do God's will, to worship God, to accept God's healing power and to be channels for it in the world. As the hymn puts it, the gold of obedience, incense of lowliness, the hope that can replace fear.

Then **the shepherds.** They were in their day people on the margins, not rated very highly by others at all. They must have gone back to their flocks filled with joy that they mattered so much to God that they were chosen to be the first witnesses of the arrival of this child. I wonder if they talked about how sad it is that people have taken so long to learn to value others, especially those on the edges of society.

Mary has often been misunderstood, made to appear too good to be true. I wonder if Mary talked with Joseph about how she wished people could understand that she was asked to do in a particular way what all of us are asked to do: bring Jesus into the world. And Joseph, who doesn't say a word in the Gospel stories would probably agree with her. He didn't talk about being willing to do God's will – he just got on with it.

There are **animals** in my crib set too. They don't say anything either, but they all play a part in the unfolding story. Jesus knew a lot about sheep and how to be a good shepherd. He must have seen how people valued their oxen too, because he said that keeping rules about the Sabbath was not as important as pulling an ox out of a ditch if it got into difficulties on the Sabbath. And the donkey – well, he certainly went places with Jesus.

I've got **an angel** as well – I suspect that angels are always saying to each other, 'I wish people would open their eyes and their minds and their hearts, and be alert to God's presence and activity.'

And of course, there's **the Baby.** He couldn't speak a word, although he was the word made flesh. But I think, as he is packed away, he is longing to be allowed to grow up. Next year, as the cribs are erected again, there he will be, the helpless baby, lying there in the straw with animals and humans looking on. But there's more to him than that.

Ponder and pray

Christmas Word
When he was born,
He couldn't speak a word,
That Word made flesh.
All he could do was cry

The human cry of hunger
And the need for love.
He had to learn his words
At Mary's knee and Joseph's bench;
Words of the Kingdom values
That informed their lives.
And when he spoke,
It was again Mary's Magnificat,
Turning our expectations upside down:

Good News of transformation.
God's Word, and ours
If we too give it flesh
And live Magnificat:
Meeting the human cry
Of hunger and the need for love.

(from *Watching for the Kingfisher*)

Lord, help us to grow in knowledge and understanding of your Word.